TRADITIONAL HOUSES OF
RURAL SPAIN

TRADITIONAL HOUSES OF
RURAL
SPAIN

Bill Laws

Photography by
Joaquim Castells Benosa

Abbeville Press Publishers
New York London Paris

Spain and its Provinces

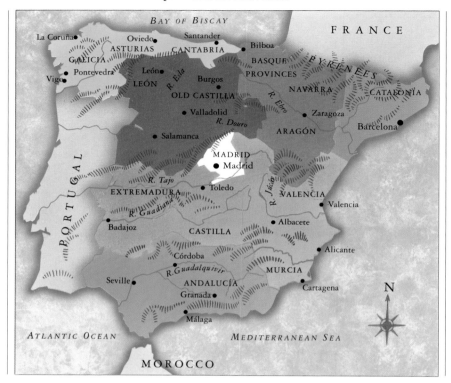

First published in the United States of America in 1995 by Abbeville Press
488 Madison Avenue New York NY 10022

First published in Great Britain in 1995 by
Collins & Brown Limited, London House, Great Eastern Wharf, Parkgate Road,
London SW11 4NQ

Copyright © Collins & Brown 1995
Text copyright © Bill Laws 1995
Photographs copyright © Joaquim Castells 1995

ISBN 0-7892-0057-0
Conceived, edited and designed by Collins & Brown
Editor Rosalynde Cossey
Senior Art Editor Ruth Hope
Art Director Roger Bristow
Maps by Andrew Farmer

HALF TITLE :
Charm from Tarragona

FRONTISPIECE :
Diverse scenery, south west of Barcelona

CONTENTS PAGE:
Spain has a hotter climate than its European neighbours and her
traditional houses reflect this. Most country buildings are small-windowed, as
well as thick-walled, designed for summer coolness and winter warmth.

  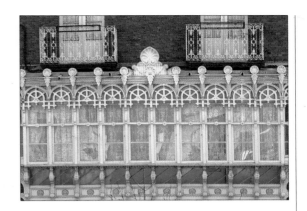

CONTENTS

$\mathcal{I}$NTRODUCTION

T HE TWO MOST AWESOME architectural monuments in Spain are the Alhambra Palace in Granada and El Escorial near Madrid. Both are born of Spanish stock, but the two stand worlds apart. Built by the Nasrid Sultans who ruled in the closing days of the Moslem occupation, the Alhambra is a masterly integration of buildings, gardens and landscape. Its plain red adobe walls, set against the snow-tipped peaks of the Sierra Nevada in southern Spain, screen a sensual architectural inner complex designed as a leisured and contemplative retreat for the Sultans.

The grey, granite magnificence of El Escorial stands in the foothills of the Guadarrama Mountains overlooking Madrid. It was designed for the Spanish King Philip II to celebrate the defeat of the French at St Quentin in 1557, but it became a mausoleum for himself and his line. Austere and solemn, El Escorial is a brooding monument to a brooding king who could not take his mind off the inevitability of death and judgement. The Christian El Escorial and the Moslem Alhambra represent two contrasting styles, two cultures and two ways of life. They also symbolise the essential and long-lasting mystery of Spain.

If we liken Spain to a rich, refined garden and its buildings to the flowers which grace the place, accidents of history have given this garden an Eden-like quality – the Mudéjar towers of northern Spain; the Moslem mosques of the south; the strange brick fortifications of Castillo de Coca in Segovia; the golden gates of Santiago de Compostela; and the flamboyant Sagrada Familia, Barcelona's shrine to 19th-century Modernismo (see Chapter 3). Other architectural plants in this cultivated garden, everyday working homes of the *sierra* (mountain ranges) and the *meseta* (the broad, elevated plains), are as celebrated as the Alhambra or El Escorial – the *pueblos blancos* (whitewashed villages) of Seville, and the windmills of La Mancha which so upset Cervantes' myopic Spanish hero, Don Quixote. Unlike the architectural masterpieces which take your breath away, these are not the

LEFT: *Farms and palaces, cottages and castles have survived for centuries hidden away deep in the Spanish countryside. No other European country possesses so much unaltered evidence of its architectural past.*

types of buildings which frighten the horses. Built of stone from the local quarries and shaded with the colours of the earth, they discreetly pattern the surrounding landscape and rarely look out of place, however bare or beautiful the terrain. The pueblos blancos brighten the barren hill sides of the southern sierra while the Romanesque *pueblos* (villages) of the high Pyrenees, medieval villages which have remained almost unchanged in four centuries, give a sense of composure to the rugged mountains.

Traditional country homes like these have been demolished and replaced with fashionable foreign imports – witness the Mediterranean coasts. Others have been neglected in an abandoned corner for so long that the earth reclaims their stones. Yet the courteous *cortijos* (farmhouses) and modest *casas* (houses), the unassuming *caseríos* (homesteads) and the humble *cabañas* (huts) which lie scattered across the high plains and mountains of Spain are the rootstock of the country's architecture. There are many guide books which detail the exotic species in the Spanish garden, but the visitor needs a sense of adventure and a traveller's eye to discover all of the folk architecture which forms the true face of Spain.

Folk architecture is a building style which lies between the primitive and the polite. In Spain, which is predominantly hotter and drier than its European neighbours, the majority of these rural buildings are thick walled and small windowed, cool in summer and warm in winter. As with any other folk art, the homes were built and furnished by local craftspeople who prudently, and from necessity, made suitable use of whatever materials lay close to hand.

In most of Spain this meant using slate or terra-cotta tiles for the roof, wood for the furniture and stone for the walls. There are pockets of fine building stone in this land of saints and boulders: alabaster in Aragón, pinkish marble in Alicante and serpentine in Almería. Venerated by its masons and carted off to shape fine city palaces and cathedrals, a little of the best stone nevertheless found its way into local country houses. Elsewhere the builder learned to work with indifferent rubble stone, or used wood, clay, *adobe* (sun dried bricks), and *tapia* or *pisé*, where coarse, sandy gravel was rammed into a petrified finish.

Romanesque in the North
ABOVE: *The Romanesque style, a blend of architectural conventions with its roots in the Roman empire, was introduced to northern Spain during the Christian conquest of the Moslems. The Spanish colonisation of the Americas further enriched the mix of architectural styles.*

Adobe and rubble stone
RIGHT: *Building methods relied on local traditions with stone, wood and earth as the basic materials. Techniques ranged from building with sun-baked bricks, the adobe of the south, to the rubble stone and slate of the north as on this Catalan house.*

The farmhouses and cottages constructed by untutored architect/builders were more than mere places in which to live. They also served to shelter the family's animals, the olive press, the cider barrels, the weaver's loom or the potter's wheel. Indeed, more room was made over to the workshop or dairy than to the family itself who had to be content with a first-floor fireside kitchen, flat-topped chest, bench, stool and basic sleeping quarters. Such a house also said something about the status of the farmer/owner. He was no less aware of contemporary styles and new materials than the land owner in his palace – he simply lacked the resources with which to express it.

The buildings which rose to meet the needs of these farmers varied from region to region. To understand why northern Pontevedra is filled with great, green granite farmhouses while southern Málaga has an abundance of whitewashed houses, or why the walls of Salamanca in the west should glow with golden limestone while houses near Tarragona in the east are built of stones as big as barrels, we need to know something of the climate, the place and the people.

Different landscapes give rise to different vernacular styles. There are half-timbered houses in the forests, snow-proof chalets in the mountains, mud and reed-thatched cabins on the moorlands, and flat-roofed cottages along the Mediterranean coast. Spain's sea shores and sierra, marshland and meseta possess an incomparable geographical variety and, consequently, an exceptional range of vernacular styles.

The weather-worn teeth of the Spanish sierra - the Spanish use the same word for both a saw and a mountain - and meseta, stripped of their forests years ago, make Spain the most mountainous country in Europe after Switzerland. Most of Spain's fifty million visitors a year come to enjoy the varied coastline which ranges from Galicia's windswept Cabo Finisterre, heading into the Atlantic and once thought to be the end of the world, to the *costa* (long beachy stretches) which shelve into the blue Mediterranean Sea. Spain has marshlands, including the National Park of Doñana in the south west, desert plains in Aragón and even, close by Olot in Catalonia, dormant volcanoes. These distinctive landscapes are scattered over 518,000 square kilometres (200,000 square miles) of fifteen mainland regions.

Arabic influences

RIGHT: *The accidents of history enriched Spanish architecture. One crucial ingredient was the eighth-century Moslem occupation which left an indelible mark on the villages of Andalucía. The Moslem Mozárabe and Mudéjar styles continued to influence the buildings of Spain long after the Moslems were defeated in 1492.*

The people themselves are as diverse as the materials and the methods of building in each region. A Castilian is no more a typical Spaniard than the flamenco is a typical Spanish dance. The people of Spain incorporate many others. Iberians drifted over from Africa to settle in the south and east, and Celts settled in the north and west. Successive waves of settlers included Greeks, Phoenicians, Carthaginians and Romans. The Basques were already a race apart and had their own language and distinctive building styles, while the Gallegos, part Celt and part Roman, and the Catalonians, of Iberian, French and Roman ancestry, were developing their own mother tongues as well as their own building techniques.

Traditional building methods are not immune to outside influences, and conquest and colonisation have added new ingredients to the vernacular mix. When the Romans invaded and settled Hispania, as they called it, the country flourished, learned and developed under Latin rule. Some feats of Roman engineering not only survive but still operate today: a spectacular Roman aqueduct continues to feed Segovia's water supply; Emperor Trajan's

Folk architecture

LEFT: *The vernacular tradition lies midway between the primitive and the polite, and serves as the rootstock of both. Like any folk art, it is a dynamic and creative expression of a people's character.*

bridge, built over the River Tagus (Río Tajo) in 106 AD, carries its daily payload to this day. Elsewhere in Spain, ashlar stone and faded Roman brick tiles are still being unearthed in the ancient walls of remote farmhouses.

When the Romans departed, the barbarian invasions swept through the country until the last of the invading hordes, the Germanic Visigoths, worked their way south from France, bringing their Visigothic styles which survive in the north of the country. The Visigoths were met and repelled by the Moslems, who remained in Spain for almost eight centuries until the Christian reconquest eventually expelled them from Andalucía. By then Spain had become the meeting point of two radically different civilisations, and nothing since has matched the impact, and the integration, of these two cultures on Spanish arts, crafts and architecture.

The Moslems were driven out in 1492, the same year in which Christopher Columbus sailed from Andalucía to search for a maritime short-cut to India but stumbled on the Americas instead. During the later colonisation, Spain flourished and enriched itself on plundered gold from these new possessions. All through the sixteenth century, palaces, religious buildings and universities materialised from the drawing boards of architects, many of whom hurried from France and Burgundy, Holland, Germany, Italy and England to share the spoils of conquest. Ironworkers, masons, sculptors, glass workers, silversmiths and ceramicists, fighting for a foothold in this new lucrative market, followed the architects and brought their influences and expertise to bear on the buildings of Spain.

No other European country possesses so much unaltered evidence of a medieval or Renaissance past, but the most pervasive influence on traditional buildings dates back to the Islamic conquest. Materials, landscapes and people helped shape the face of the traditional houses of rural Spain. Since the essential ingredients differ from region to region, from valley to valley, subtle differences, mixed like a finely blended sherry, led to a rich end result. Old habits die hard; it is still quite possible to sit outside the village café on a fine spring day and watch a householder mixing mortar and constructing some more of his own walls in exactly the same way as his grandfather's grandfather did before him.

CHAPTER ONE

GALICIA, ASTURIAS AND CANTABRIA

THE UNDULATING HILLS of Galicia, Asturias and Cantabria lie wedged between the mountains of the Cordillera Cantábrica and the Atlantic Ocean forming a landscape where, it is said, the grass meets the sea. Galicia is the Celtic stronghold of Spain, a green region of moss-covered granite, deep forests, secretive *rías* – the fjord-like coves caused by the Atlantic Ocean nibbling away at its eastern coastline – and the site of one of the most beautiful cities in Spain, Santiago de Compostela.

The Galicians speak their own language, Gallego, enjoy their own music, respect their own superstitions, feast on their own cuisine and build their own distinctive houses. They are often compared to Bretons, the Irish, and the Welsh, but unlike their Celtic counterparts, they enjoy real summer warmth between showers. Small farms, allotments fenced off with slabs of slate and *hórreos* (granite granaries) decorated with saints and crosses, show a peculiarly Galician character.

Hórreos of a different design, but still placed on table-shaped supports or staddle stones to keep rats at bay, are also a traditional feature of the countryside around Galicia's neighbours, Asturias and Cantabria. The Costa Verde (Green Coast) of Asturias and its mountainous hinterland, slit and riven by hidden river valleys, lie between the Rivers Eo in the west and Deva in the east. Inland, the soaring Picos de Europa separate the province from neighbouring Castilla to the south and Cantabria to the east.

The Asturian kings maintained an isolated bastion of Christianity here in the ninth and tenth century and founded a singular collection of Pre-Romanesque village churches, superior by far to those of their Christian contemporaries anywhere else in Europe. The same kings presided over some complex local customs and traditions which have survived them by a thousand years, preserved partly by the region's self-sufficiency in fishing,

Part of the landscape

LEFT: *Built from the groundstones beneath their foundations, the traditional rural buildings of Spain rarely look out of place however bare or beautiful the terrain.*

15

Small is beautiful

LEFT: *Celtic Galicia and its neighbouring regions of Asturias and Cantabria are patterned by small farms, small villages and curious granaries like these in Coruña province near Cabo Finisterre.*

Houses and hórreos

LEFT: *A Galician farmhouse and its outbuilding overlook the Atlantic in the green pastureland of La Coruña. This is the land where they say the grass meets the sea and where maize, introduced by the* Americanos, *has become an indispensable crop.*

as well as farming, forestry and mining, and partly by the mountain chain which isolated the region from the rest of Spain. Neighbouring Cantabria shares with Asturias the incongruous sight of twentieth-century trucks piled with mined ore lumbering past medieval ox carts loaded with fresh farm produce for the miners' market. In the Cantabrian hinterland hay may be harvested with a sickle and loaded with wooden pitch forks on to old carts, but the *pueblos malditos*, the 'damned villages' as they are sometimes sardonically called by outsiders, evoke more than a trace of envy for their sounds of quiet country life – the ringing of cow bells and the clatter of clogs on cobbles.

The architectural thread running through these three regions and their neighbours to the east consists of the Camino de Santiago, the once dusty lanes and dangerous highways north and south of the Cordillera Cantábrica that wound their way through the countryside to the great golden towers of the Cathedral of Santiago de Compostela. In the early days of pilgrimage to the shrine of Saint James the Apostle, it was customary for the first in the pilgrim party who glimpsed the Santiago towers to be awarded the title

Painted galerías

RIGHT: *The balcony is an essential feature of any traditional Spanish house. The climate in Galicia is mild and temperate and the rainfall abundant. The practice of panelling and glazing the balcony protected the householder from the elements.*

Symbolic shell

RIGHT: *The image of the scallop, an allusion to the Knights of Santiago who adopted the shell as their symbol, appears on buildings across Spain. Here the side of a house in the province of Pontevedra is weatherproofed with a chain mail of the real thing, nailed to timbers.*

'king', a surname he could use for the rest of his life; the Galician phone book is full of the family name Rey, Spanish for 'king'. Today as then, the pilgrims bow to touch foreheads with the carved bust of Maestro Mateo, a widely known stonemason of the Romanesque age. It is an appropriate act of respect, for it was Mateo and other craftsmen of his ilk who moulded the look of these northern buildings.

Granite is the master stone of Galicia. It is carved into monolithic lintels or framed into giant blocks around doors and windows, their sizes being highlighted by the local practice of keeping them free of whitewash when painting and repainting the walls. Galicia experiences much bad weather

and granite was the preferred material to meet it, in the lighthouses and quays and in the farms and wayside villages of the Camino de Santiago.

Saint James (Santiago Matamoros) the Moslem slayer is said to have appeared in battle alongside Christians, and slaughtered not only Arabs but also the unfortunate American Indians of the New World. His shrine led to monasteries, chapels and hostels springing up along the Camino as hordes of outsiders penetrated on foot and horseback into deepest Cantabria, Asturias and Galicia.

During the twelfth century, at the invitation of the Castilian king, the colonising Cistercians carried out their own invasion and built more than sixty monasteries including those at Osera, Melón, Meira and Oya. Their emissary St Bernard, championing the virtues of poverty and railing against the increasingly decorative style of the architectural arts, demanded to know: 'What use are these ridiculous monsters, these ferocious lions, centaurs, tigers and soldiers, in places where monks devote themselves to study?' His Order sent architects from the mother monastery, Clairvaux in Burgundy, to ensure that the locals did not meddle with the aesthetics his mission preferrred. This tactic did not always work. In particular, local craftsmen left their distinctive mark on the great doors of the western porch of one of the most Burgundian of monasteries, Meira, high in the sierra north east of Lugo. The ironwork hinges look like giant metal centipedes crushed against the seasoned wood and embellished and engraved with what would have been regarded as a scandalous amount of decoration.

Cistercian monks had little to teach the Galicians about poverty. The small agricultural holdings which patterned the four provinces – Orense, Lugo, Coruña and Pontevedra – endured a subsistence economy with much use of barter; such systems continue in some country areas. At O Cebreiro, and at Cervantes and Donís in the protective folds of the mountainous Los Ancares National Reserve at Villarello, the villagers maintain their ancient *pallozas*, circular huts built of granite, topped with conical thatched roofs, and grouped in *castros*, fortified hilltop villages. Some, with windowless interiors, straw-covered floors and bare stone walls, have been converted to serve as *refugios*, simple bunkhouse accommodation for young pilgrims

Timber frame

RIGHT: *Seasoned timbers frame the window opening in the rubble stone walls of a barn roofed with flag stone in the Lugo province. Wooden shutters like these served as the basic fenestration for many of Galicia's mountain homes.*

Thatcher's craft
RIGHT: *The design of the hórreo
varied from region to region and village
to village across northern Spain.
Here in the mountains of the Cordillera
Cantábrica the hórreo was placed on
staddle stones to keep out
rats and mice.*

walking to Santiago. Such round dwellings are rooted in the Bronze Age
and are among the oldest house types in Europe. There were disadvantages
in living in low, circular rooms and having to share your living space with
your animals, but these were outweighed by the fact that these tent-like
buildings were cheap and simple to construct. They had no cornerstones
and no chimney; the wood smoke simply curled out through an opening in
the thatch. Today, they are used for storage or, as at O Cebreiro, form a
national monument. Their survival is indicative of the endemic poverty
these country people have frequently endured.

The appearance of a countryside at peace with itself masks a centuries'
old problem: Pontevedra, Compostela, Lugo and other townships in the area
were never large enough to sustain the population despite the 30,000 or so
little hamlets in Galicia. Consequently, emigration was a priority for young
people and there was constant traffic of Gallegos to Latin America, most
particularly to Argentina — the Gallegos call Buenos Aires their fifth
province. However, a people who built such elaborate hórreos that many

Mountain alleyway

RIGHT: *The narrow, covered alleyway in this mountain village threads its way between the bare stone walls of the buildings. The slate-like rocks were cut and laid with the larger stones at the base of the walls and the smaller ones at the top.*

Thatched pallozas

LEFT: *The pallozas are among the earliest homes on the Iberian mainland. The best of the hand-hewn granite was reserved for the door and window surrounds. These ancient pallozas are still used in the mountain borderlands.*

Graced with granite

LEFT: *The Galicians speak their own language, thought to be the mother of Portuguese, and come from Celtic stock. Strong religious links with the rest of Catholic Spain were forged by the founding of the shrine of Saint James at Santiago de Compostela.*

pilgrims to Compostela mistook them for hermitages could not be described as lacking the necessities of the good life. It was enough to persuade many ex-migrants to return, building themselves new bungalows in Ortigueira and other hamlets where the whitewashed stone cottages stand out against a green woodland backcloth, or settling in the refurbished *pazos* (manor houses) which lie along the river valleys of Pontevedra.

The Galician gentry were fond of country life and their former *casas fuertes* (fortified houses) were turned into comfortable pazos, from where the country estate could be managed. When the tenant farmers paid their tithes of maize, meat or potatoes, the produce was stored in cellars and barns in close proximity to the house.

Wrought-iron gates adorned with family coronets opened on to avenues of chestnuts and lime trees, the houses behind them decorated with formal family portraits, hunting trophies and damask curtains, Gardens were laid out with neat hedges separating the *huerto de verduras* (vegetable garden)

Stone-faced balcony

RIGHT: *Here stone slabs have been split and cut into sections which could be slotted into grooves in the balcony timbers to provide a wind-proof wall. The contrasting shades of stone and weathered paint give an elemental charm to these old hillside houses.*

Rain-proof roof

RIGHT: *The stones on these hipped roofs were carefully graded with the smaller slabs near the ridge and the larger ones at the eaves. The overhanging eaves let the snow fall free of the house. Corrugated tin has replaced the stone on many of these mountain houses.*

from the pear and apple orchards and meadow grazing land. The family would congregate at the pazo for the summer months and occupy the upper floors; the ground floor accommodated the servants' quarters, weaving and carpentry workshops, the bakery, the *bodega* (wine cellar) and all the other necessities of life needed to maintain the family in the style to which they were accustomed. Another favourite place to settle was among the vineyards of Cambados, home of the fresh, young Albariño wine thought to have been imported to Pontevedra by pilgrims from Cluny.

In Cambados, as in Orense and Lugo, whole villages were built of solid granite, their long, low roofs spreading out across first-floor balconies. The balcony is a necessary addition to any Spanish building, and villages throughout the country hold annual competitions for the best-tended house verandah or balcony. Even in the windswept parts of Galicia, the balcony serves both as a place to dry maize cobs and as somewhere to sit with a glass of fiery orujo in the evening. Balconies reached a high point in their development with the seafront *galerías* or *solanas acristaladas*, the glass-fronted houses where whole walls of verandahs are glazed against the sea spray, most commonly in La Coruña, from which port Philip II's ill-fated armada set sail in 1588 carrying many Galician sailors to their deaths. Few country people enjoyed the luxury of windows, let alone glass. Where windows were let into the thick masonry walls, they were more often sealed with pigskin, which was transparent, or a simple wooden shutter than a sheet of glass.

Three of Galicia's provinces face the Atlantic, so house builders had to ensure that their roofs as well as their windows were wind- and weather-tight. The people of Miño used woven straw to make *corozas* (waterproof capes), and wood to fashion their *zuecos*, the high shoes worn in the rainy season to keep out the wet. On roofs, slate rather than terra-cotta tiles was employed to keep out the rain. Actually, the use of slate was widespread, in the Cordillera Cantábrica right through to Cantabria where it also served for steps, salting benches, floors, fences and panels, and sometimes on the weather side of coastal houses. Scallop shells, (see Chapter Five) in typical vernacular tradition, replaced slate where the latter proved too expensive. In Galicia, each wave that washes the rocky shores is said to represent the soul

Vineyard cottages
RIGHT: *Wine growers' houses, their pointing picked out in whitewash, sit on the vineyard terraces near Orense. Wine-making was brought to Galicia by the Romans who named the region after the Celtic tribes, the Gallaeci.*

of a lost sailor, and fate and superstition go hand in hand. Among the lace makers' white-washed cottages in Muxía on the Costa de la Muerte, (coast of death), the humble *vieira* (scallop) was seen as a symbol of the world – the sun in its lines, the earth in its hardness and the sea in its origins. The earliest known representation of the scallop, adopted by the Knights of the Order of Santiago and later emblazoned on the façades of religious buildings across Spain, is carved on the wall of the little church of Pola de Lena near Oviedo in neighbouring Asturias.

The Asturians not only prevented the Moslems from conquering their capital Cangas de Onís, east of Oviedo, but can claim to live in the region where the Christian nation of Spain was reborn. Alkama, a Moslem general, was beaten back at the mountain glen of Covadonga in the Picos de Europa by Don Pelayo the leader of a band of Christian guerrillas; these deep and impenetrable mountains then witnessed the first forays of the reconquest which eventually led to the expulsion of the Moslems.

The jagged karst peaks of the Picos de Europa were given their name by weary mariners grateful for a glimpse of the snow-white summits as they returned from their travels. They are the most awe-inspiring of the Cordillera Cantábrica, rising higher than 2,600 metres (8,500 feet). They shelter not only the chamois, the wolf and the odd bear, but also the almost mystical Vaqueros. These people were marginalised from Asturian society, banned even from burying their dead in consecrated ground. This may be why they retained their migratory customs and protected their thatched pallozas for so long. Wintering their precious cattle in the old whaling port of Luarca and other lowland towns, they departed for the mountains in spring, following the retreating snow line, their possessions stacked in trundling ox carts, and resting with their animals in pallozas on the way. They drove their sheep deep into the mountains until they gained the *brañas* (grazing lands) and the tiny thatch and stone hamlets which survive at, among other places, La Pornacal in the Somiedo National Reserve. As the bad weather of autumn closed in, they made their way back down to the Costa Verde, Luarca or Ribadesella where the mountains form a dramatic backdrop to the old, red-tiled houses.

Water source

ABOVE: *Communal springs still serve the villagers in some remote rural areas. No expense was spared on the stone surrounds for this one at Allariz near Orense, the provincial capital which is famous for its hot springs.*

Wooded frame

LEFT: *A timber screen ventilates the produce stored in this barn at Celorio. Practical solutions like these often produced striking vernacular features which were repeated in the neighbourhood.*

Curtain of corn

RIGHT: *A screen of maize dries on the balcony of a typical Asturian casa at Celorio on the Costa Verde. The stone and timber columns carry the weight of the balcony and the terra-cotta tile roof above.*

Clay tiles roof the Asturian hórreos which are constructed as rectangular wooden shrines and roofed with red tiles. On village houses, small boulders line the ridge and eaves of the roofs to hold down the tiles, and the roofs are jettied out to shelter the typical terraces beneath. In Potes they follow a tradition of building their balconies on first-floor ceiling joists, run out through the walls. Elsewhere an upstairs balcony with a sheltered terrace below are created by building the side walls of the house out like a pair of cart horse blinkers. Centre posts, sometimes carved into a modest imitation of a Romanesque church pillar, support the balcony and roof. The working life of the farmer centred on the ground floor, while home life revolved around the first floor where the walls were given a cheerful green or red limewash and the wooden handrails of the balcony were decorated with simple and skilful carvings.

One of the most widespread elements of all Spanish decorative art was the roof tile. Called Spanish tiles by northern Europeans, the Moslems introduced them to the country in the seventh or eighth centuries. Tapered towards one end, the early tiles took the shape of the tile maker's thigh. Later they were made in their thousands as tapered clay cylinders, turned on foot-powered potter's wheels and cut in twos to make pairs. Bedded in clay or mortar, the tiles were laid locked together, one row facing up, one row facing down, the taper preventing the tile from slipping from the roof. There were, however, practical disadvantages to using tiles. Tiles could be laid on a shallow pitched roof, and rocks could be placed strategically to secure any loose tiles. However, this technique was impractical for roofing complicated gables and dormers, so the house builders kept their broad-hipped roofs as plain and simple as possible. Tile colours depended on the heat of the firing and the quality of the clay. Different shades of terra-cotta in combination with the effects of light on these serpentine surfaces still make their memorable impact on the appearances of Spanish houses.

Cantabria claims to have the highest number of cows in Europe; since many of these animals used the lower quarters of the houses, the doorways were built as broad as the house cow's hind quarters; the doorways were also framed with whitewash as an aid to finding the door in the dark. West of

Mule trains

LEFT: *Spain is home to many marginalised people, some as famous as Maragatos, muleteers who carted goods from Castile over the Montes de León to Galicia. Houses here in Castrillo de los Polvazares were built back from the road on which the mule trains passed.*

Colours of Castile

BELOW: *Nine months of winter and three months of hell is the cynic's view of the Castillian climate. Whatever the weather, the bright blast of a brilliant door brings bold colour to local façades.*

In the north, the Cordillera Cantábrica and the Montes de León separate Galicia and Asturias from León, Palencia and Burgos. To the south, the Sierra de Gredos and Sierra de Guadarrama divide Castilla y León from its southern neighbours, Cáceres in Extremadura and Toledo, and Guadalajara in Castilla La Mancha. The mountain passes of the Iberian Cordillera in the east are regularly blocked by snow in winter, cutting off the foothill villages of Soria from their neighbours on the Ebro plains in La Rioja and Aragón.

In spring the meltwaters fill the rushing streams and glacial lakes of these hills in a thaw which feeds the source of the Duero, Castilla y León's major artery. The river soaks up the supplies of more than fifty tributaries on its westerly journey towards Oporto in Portugal. It is said that the Duero drinks all the waters. But without the river, its tributaries and elaborate irrigation systems this parched land would have turned to desert long ago. Instead, the arable plains support a sweep of wheat, oats and rye in an ocean of grain stretching from horizon to horizon, a vista which is broken

Christian hallmark

BELOW: *Decorative ironwork was a hallmark of Christian Castille and no cathedral door or palace portal was complete without some sturdy example of the iron craft. The decorated nail heads, key hole plate and door handle were all the work of the village smith.*

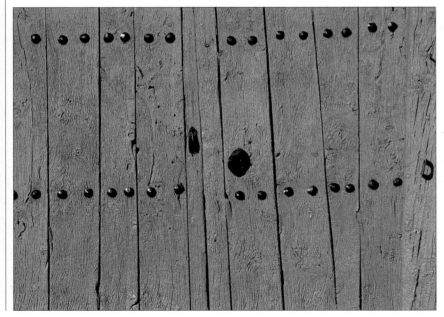

La Alberca

LEFT: *In the foothills of the Sierra de la Peña de Francia at La Alberca, where the land is farmed by hand and by mule and the view overlooks the great bull-breeding plains of Salamanca, the houses have a ground floor of ashlar stone and overhanging upper floors of timber.*

only by the occasional sight of forlorn and half-deserted villages. Early Iberian communities established their farming settlements along the Duero until the Roman conquerors systematically wiped them out. During the legendary siege of Numancia in Soria, the last Spanish settlement to fall to Rome, the people burned the town and themselves rather than submit to Roman rule. Most of the Roman remains have long been quarried and borne away for their stone, but the simple elegant aqueduct in the city of Segovia was preserved because it carried the city's water supply.

Throughout the tenth and eleventh centuries, Castile was a frontier state with local warlords battling for supremacy, not only against the Moslems, but against each other. The occupying Arabs swept back and forth across Castile as Christian Spain gradually emerged in Asturias, spreading down over the mountains of the Cordillera Cantábrica and on into the central meseta. As the Christian capital transferred from Cangas de Onís, near Oviedo in Asturias, to León, regional building methods fell under the spell of the Mozárabes, the Christian refugees who fled the south bringing their Mozarabic styles with them.

Both Christians and Arabs built defensive networks of castles, the designs based on those of the earlier castles in Andalucía. In the south, the castle builders used tapia or pisé for their monumental rectangular walls; in the north, the rubble stone was of too poor a quality to form neat corners, so circular or semi-circular towers were built. However, as the Christians recaptured Moslem lands and enslaved the skilled Mudéjar bricklayers, they put their slaves to work on a new generation of castles and churches.

One of the most extraordinary results was the fifteenth-century pink brick battlements of Castillo de Coca, built in Segovia by Mudéjar slaves for Don Alfonse de Fonseca, a spectacularly wealthy archbishop of Seville. For all its apparent military might, the rose-coloured brick disguised a soaring construction built more for effect than strength.

Rodrigo Díaz de Vivar, known to the Moslems as El Cid, was born around 1043 near Burgos and died in Valencia in 1099. A heroic soldier whose legendary exploits led to his portrayal as a virtuous knight of Arthurian proportions, El Cid was the son of one of the many families who

97

Farming community

LEFT: *The great double doors of the houses, built high and wide to take a mule and cart, indicate the agricultural origins of La Alberca. The half-timbered upper storeys lie hidden beneath a layer of stucco, the thin but durable plaster invented in Italy in the fifteenth century.*

ruled Castile through the Middle Ages. In Pedraza, to the east of Segovia, medieval walls surround a manorial village where the manor houses of pale ashlar are crusted with escudos de armas, and the tall, balconied windows overlook streets paved with pebbles.

No sooner had El Cid and his successors reclaimed their land from the Moslems than French Benedictines from Cluny moved in. The Benedictines had ensured the international success of the pilgrimage of Santiago de Compostela, placing their Romanesque stamp of approval on monasteries, hospices and churches which lined the Camino on either side of the Cordillera Cantábrica. Now they followed the Reconquest, reorganising the Spanish church and setting the seal of four full centuries of French influence on Spanish architecture.

Astorga, Ponferrada, León, Sahagún and Burgos were all located on the line of the southern Camino de Santiago as it passed from La Rioja to Santiago de Compostela. Romanesque clearly influenced the churches and old houses of these towns and villages, as it did the northern side of the Cordillera Cantábrica.

The old Roman version of classical style persisted in the western Roman empire and, with the rise of Christianity, became the basis of the Romanesque. The Romanesque would eventually develop firstly as Gothic and later, through Italian architecture, as Renaissance in a revival of the early classical styles.

The Leonese masons who carved the Romanesque foliage on the capitals of columns supporting the roof of the crypt in the church of San Isidoro in León, as well as the fresco painters who worked their pigments into the wet plaster of its roof to depict vivid scenes of rural life would have been pleased by their day-to-day work. They may not have recognised their handiwork as an exceptional piece of Romanesque art.

The money which paid their wages, and added to the ascendancy of the monastic rule, was derived from the backs of merino sheep. The flocks, led by their shepherds and followed by a plume of dust, moved like a restless sea of wool along the *cañadas*, the grazing routes of the meseta which were once marked out with lines of canes. Famous for their fine wool, merino

Hand of hospitality
ABOVE: *The willowy Hand of Fatíma was a symbol of Moslem sympathy. Adopted across Spain as a graceful design for a door knocker, it served as another example of the ironmaster's art, seen here on a village door at Candelario in Salamanca.*

sheep were descendants of a strain developed during the Roman regime. They are as adaptable to the open ranges of Texas and the vast outback of Australia as they are to the Castilian meseta. Their fleeces are heavy in oil, their lambs small and slow growing, and their flocks tolerate travelling long distances under a hard sun before reaching food and water.

In the fourteenth and fifteenth century immense flocks of merino were driven to Medina del Campo, between Salamanca and Valladolid, for the sheep fairs. Medina has fine though faded buildings and remains a busy agricultural market. In the Middle Ages it attracted wool merchants from across Europe – they bought the wool cheap, took it home to be woven and sold the cloth back to the Castilians at a good profit.

In the early-sixteenth century when some semblance of political unity was finally established, Spain under Castilian rule began gradually to amass a sprawling empire which included Naples, Sardinia, Sicily, Germany, Austria, part of eastern France, the Low Countries and the Americas. By the time the melancholic King Philip II reached the throne in 1556, settling on Madrid as the capital, Castilla y León was already being bled dry to pay the costs of the empire's upkeep.

The region never quite recovered. In 1500 the population was three times the size of today's and although transhumant shepherds still stroll their flocks along the trailing cañadas, the faded architectural treasures and crumbling castillos of small Castilian towns and the depopulated pueblos are all benchmarks of this once great state.

Merino wool money and, later, Third World gold, was lavished on the high architecture of Castilla y León. Most of the celebrated architects of the fifteenth century were foreigners and they oversaw the succession of civic and religious buildings which rose above town and village houses. There was a tendency to hide sumptuous and affluent interiors behind solid, almost austere exteriors and El Escorial, the final fling of a tottering empire, seemed to symbolise the profligacy. Hailed as the eighth wonder of the world when completed in 1584, it took 1500 workers a comparatively brief twenty-one years to build the 300 rooms, hang 1200 doors and glaze 2,600 windows. It stood as a gargantuan monument to King Philip II, to

Candelario

ABOVE: *Householders in Candelario, high up in the Sierra de Gredos kept the stonework around the doors and windows free of whitewash. They protected their doors with flood gates, closed against the snow meltwater which rushed down the steep maze of paved lanes in early spring.*

Tar-painted timbers

RIGHT: *These sensitively restored houses, their timbers tarred for protection against the elements, stand in the old quarter of Covarrubias on the banks of the river Arlanza south of Burgos.*

the highly influential architect Juan de Herrera and, of course, also to the sixteenth-century Spanish extravagance.

The excesses of El Escorial were not lost on the domestic buildings of Castilla y León. Accustomed to living in their baronial fortresses, the feuding medieval nobility were happier with imposing buildings of huge squared ashlar blocks as tall and wide as they were long. There was still an inclination to build citadel-like towers at the corners of the buildings and incorporate parapets which looked like battlements, despite the fact that the most hostile visitor was likely to be the village debt collector.

Almost as an afterthought, these palaces might acquire an elaborate doorway, dripping with finely carved decoration or effervescent, lace-like plasterwork. Indoors, the ground floor would be given over to stabling, and the top floor to servants' quarters while the family occupied the various rooms of the first floor – *salones* (drawing-rooms and dining-rooms), and bedrooms with scrubbed wooden floors and artesonado ceilings. In the Moslem manner, a medieval town or country house often enclosed an inner courtyard, a feature which was the forerunner of the Spanish patio.

The Gothic influence, adopted and adapted to Castilian tastes, led to wide-arched doorways and rectangular mouldings framing the doors and windows. The Spanish zest for embellishment was irresistible. Mouldings on one palace in Zamora were shaped like the knotted cord belt of the Franciscan Order to which the house once belonged. On the Casa de las Conchas (House of Shells) in Salamanca, the walls were decorated with stone scallops, symbol of the Knights of the Order of Santiago. A grand mirador, styled like an Italian loggia, was built as a gallery on the front of the building, and inside the Casa, as in many of the Castilian palaces, an inner patio was surrounded by a two-storey arcade.

A significant number of older, grander houses possessed only one storey for living accommodation. Second or third storeys were added only after the repeal of the law requiring the owners of houses more than one storey high to place half their home and its furniture at the disposal of the court. When the court moved to Valladolid in 1600, many built themselves single-storey Casas de la Malicia (literally, houses of wickedness), in an enterprising effort

Storey story

ABOVE: *Householders were penalised if their homes were more than one storey high. Consequently many single-storey* casas de la malicia *(literally, houses of wickedness) were built.*

Colour coordination

RIGHT: *Country colours in Castile were drawn from the raw earth, from burnt sienna browns to yellow ochres, set off here by a strongly contrasting blind. Rural houseowners were far more adventurous with their colours than they are today.*

Manorial seat
LEFT: *The gift of a feudal estate and mansion were traditional rewards for loyalty to the Christian crown and bravery against the Moslems. At Pedraza, east of Segovia, manorial houses like these were built of pale ashlar and decorated with family coats of arms or blasones.*

to circumvent the law from which only widows, the clergy and the poor were exempt – not that any monarch in his or her right mind would be tempted to share half the impoverished home of the meseta shepherd.

The country people built simple homes to protect themselves from the searing heat of summer and the bitter cold of winter and they continue to live in these adobe houses in remote pueblos, following the centuries-old cycle of hard work, exhausted rest and fervent prayer. Today they are as philosophical about the eclipsed fortunes of a once world-famous region as they are about the few bemused tourists who stray into the old territories. They reserve their passions for market place arguments about the qualities of the autumn *vendimia* (grape harvest), or the relative merits of the gallant broad-shouldered *toros bravos* (fighting bulls).

Country families manage with a small cabaña, built of adobe, roofed with cast-off tiles and warmed by iron brasiers filled with smouldering olive

Palace life

RIGHT: *Settling on lands captured from the Moslems, the new Christian rulers followed the fashions of the north, building imposing palaces in imitation of El Escorial. Inside, these buildings often contained Moslem features such as peaceful inner courtyards and elaborate artesonado ceilings.*

Simple life

LEFT: *Many country Castellanos still follow the centuries-old cycle of work, rest and prayer, from necessity as much as from choice. Methods of transport, like methods of building, have changed little over the centuries.*

Spyhole

BELOW: *Having vanquished the Moslems, Catholic Spain adopted many of their architectural features such as the reja or window grille. The spy hole was used to detect unwelcome visitors.*

branches hung from the underside of the kitchen table. Covered with a table cloth which reached down to the tiled floor, the table might be laid with *barro cocido*, glazed earthenware.

If, as many did, the son of the family moved out of the village and then profited from such enterprise, he might expect to settle his family into a small town house where the rooms were heated by a decent log fire, the smouldering wood propped up on *morillos* (firedogs). The family could view arcaded streets framed by the iron window grille, the reja, which covered every lower floor window then and now.

Although the iron reja was believed to cool the hot air entering the house, shutters, often fitted with a small hinged panel, performed the task far more effectively. Spanish windows invariably open inward and those in the upper floors were tucked in under the broad eaves of the roof to shade them from the harsh, bleaching midday sun. Castile, however, is not an inhospitable expanse of meseta, baked dry in summer, frozen in winter.

Merino sheep

BELOW: *Much of the money used to build the fine houses of Castile came from the backs of the merino sheep. Merino sheep were famous for their fleeces, taken for sale at the international wool market of Medina del Campo.*

Declining prosperity
RIGHT: *In the middle ages, the province of Soria owed its prosperity to the Mesta, the powerful fellowship of sheep farmers who controlled the cañadas or cane-marked migration routes of the merino flocks.*

Mediterranean tile
RIGHT: *Introduced by the Moslems, the terra-cotta tile was eventually adopted across southern Europe. The quality of the clay and heat of the firing dictated the colour of the tile while its shape was only suitable for broad, hipped roofs like these.*

Zamora, once a base for both the Roman and the Moslem settlers (the name comes from Ciudad Mora, meaning Moslem town), was built on the great Duero River and the surrounding countryside was neatly divided between the rolling, productive wheat fields of the Tierra del Pan (land of bread), while the southern Tierra del Vino was given over, as the name suggests, to viniculture. Northern Zamora, like north-western León, backs up into the mountains which provided rough mountain stone and schist, stone which could be split into thin, irregular plates to wall and roof the houses and shelter the characteristic wooden balconies.

Ponferrada west of León, named after its iron ballustraded bridge, is the modern mining centre of El Bierzo where money was made from mining as far back as Roman times. Modern Bercianos speak Gallego and would prefer their area to be counted as Galicia's fifth province. The ancient Romans washed out more than 900,000 kilograms (885 tons) of gold from the land; today's Bercianos extract coal, cobalt and iron.

Changing faces
RIGHT: *Traditional rural buildings,
like the people, change with the times
and these houses in Soria show the
gradual transition from the vernacular
towards the polite. The house in the
foreground with its stone columns and
'French' windows would have been
considered superior to its
neighbour next door.*

French influence
RIGHT: *French Benedictines brought
the Romanesque to Spain and centuries
later the fashionable town houses were
still imitating Gallic styles. Here the
old windows have been replaced with
tall French windows.*

South east of Ponferrada was La Maragatería, homeland of the *maragatos* (muleteers) who, until the railways put them out of business, made a living from transporting goods from Castile through the oak forests and groves of walnuts and chestnuts to Galicia. Country houses in the main streets of many villages such as Castrillo de los Polvazares, close to the Maragatos' capital, Astorga, were built well back from the broad highway to allow the passage of the mule trains.

As supplies of usable freestone dwindled further south, the builder used mortar to hold together the irregular stones. In Segovia especially, the habit grew of highlighting the pointing, reinforcing it with small pebbles or limewashing the mortar and leaving the stone bare. This led to *esgrafiado*, the practice of drawing out decorative designs in the plaster and cement on a wall's surface.

In the provinces of Palencia and Burgos, the character of the countryside changes again. Frómista's church of San Martin was intended to be the most perfect example of Romanesque architecture in Spain; just beyond it is a covey of circular dovecotes. Pigeon has always been an important source of winter meat and few old farmhouses were built without pigeon lofts. The

Battle zone

LEFT: *Emerging from its role as a battle zone between Christian and Moslem, Castilla y León became part of the political heart of Spain. Castellano was adopted as the national language and Castilian rulers governed a vast empire. It did not last.*

agricultural plains of these northern lands give way to lonely canyons cut out of the limestone massifs by the River Ebro. Small orchards and riverside gardens surrounded the villages here and in southern Burgos where there used to be enough wood for building purposes.

The humorous explanation for the lack of trees in Castile was that because birds ate the crops and lived in the trees, if you cut down all the trees you would have fine crops! A more convincing explanation was the voracious appetite for ship-building timber, as well as the equally voracious grazing habits of the merino sheep.

In places like Palenzuela and Covarrubias south of Burgos, the wood was used with economy because of its expense and increasing scarcity. The broadest timbers were reserved for the rectangular frame and the panels of the building filled with sapling-sized supports, spaced wide apart. Jettied out across the pavement, the upper storeys of the buildings rest on timber or stone columns and keep the pavement in the shade. At La Alberca, high up in the remote hills of the Sierra de la Peña de Francia south of Salamanca, the village streets wind round to the plaza where the second-floor balconies of the timber-framed houses circle the buildings like a vertiginous footpath.

Busy, exciting, cosmopolitan Madrid sits between Castilla y León and Castilla La Mancha. It is a city of nearly five million people who claim with justification that their nightlife allows them to stay up later than any other Spanish city. But even the Madrileños grow tired and it is to the pastoral backwaters of places like La Alberca that they withdraw to restore their jaded spirits.

CHAPTER FIVE

CASTILLA
LA MANCHA AND
EXTREMADURA

T HE BROAD AREA of Extremadura, Castilla La Mancha, Valencia and Murcia runs like a waistband across Spain with Madrid as the buckle in the middle. A journey across this centre ground from Portugal to the Mediterranean reveals a rolling palette of colour ranging from the dun and dark green shades of Extremadura to the fresh green of Valencia with slashes of purple saffron, yellow sunflowers and whitewashed villages in between.

Spain has at least two and a half thousand castles and about a thousand are divided between Castilla y León and Castilla La Mancha. They range from a forgotten pile of stones in some quiet corner of a country village to the magnificent fifteenth-century Guadamur Castle near Toledo and the mile-and-a-half-long city walls, fortified with 88 towers, which circle Spain's highest provincial capital Avila, over the border in Castilla y León.

After the rugged castles came the Spanish noblemen's fortified palaces and manor houses traditionally built around a courtyard and a well. Marginally further down on the social scale were imposing farmhouses, the *cigarrales* of the Toledo outskirts, built of whitewashed adobe and decorated with ceramic tiles, their reclusive inner courtyards shaded by refreshingly cool, double-decker galleries.

The workers' homes, which clustered around the bases of landowners' houses, ranged from the whitewashed and terra-cotta pink of the south to the bare, tawny brown stone of the north. Built two storeys high, but with extra storage and drying lofts under the roof, cooling breezes passed along the upper floors through the overhanging balconies. The ground floor was given over to the kitchen, living room and, in the country areas, stabling

La Mancha windmills
LEFT: *The best loved of Spain's traditional country buildings, the windmills of la Mancha, are world famous for their role in the story of Don Quixote. But the high dark sierra, the deep green olive groves and the arid meseta conceal a unique range of rural buildings.*

and workshops. In the mountains, the *arquitectura negra* (black architecture) of the dark, slate stone buildings look like rare survivors from the Middle Ages while the fourteenth-century *casas colgadas* (hanging houses) at Cuenca were so crowded together that those on the edge of the local ravine leaned alarmingly over the precipice.

The provinces of Cáceres and Badajoz lie to the west between Portugal and the central region, Castilla La Mancha. This is Extremadura, literally land beyond the Duero, a 16,000-square-mile (41,000-square-kilometre) platform of schist and granite, scented with wild thyme and eucalyptus and won back from the Moslems by the conquering kings of León.

In the days when Madrid formed part of this southern region, Castilla La Mancha was known as La Nueva, New Castile. Now that Madrid forms an autonomous province of its own, the region has become Castilla La Mancha, the dry southern meseta which took its name from the Arab manxa, the dry land. Breathlessly hot in summer and numbingly cold in winter, the land nevertheless pays its way.

The Río Tajo, which cuts its way through the karst Alcarria in Guadalajara before running through Toledo and out towards Portuguese Lisbon, together with the Río Guadiana, making its leisurely way west to Badajoz, are responsible for green acres of wheat, olives and vines which break up the bare meseta plains of the five provinces, Toledo, Ciudad Real, Guadalajara, Cuenca and Albacete.

Finally to the east is the Levante, the regions of Valencia and Murcia, which occupy the narrow but fertile alluvial belt and the inland massifs between Castilla La Mancha, Andalucía and the Mediterranean. Here the traditional crops of carob, almond, olive and vines, still watered by the ingenious irrigation systems inherited from the Romans, are supplemented by the fertile *huertas* (literally, irrigated areas) with their lemon and orange orchards, palm groves and rice paddies. Extracting the underground deposits of lead, zinc and copper, and capitalising on the seaside tourist industry have contributed to the Levante's fruitful, mixed economy.

The tourist potential of Extremadura and Castilla La Mancha has only recently begun to be exploited. Even the granite palaces decorated with

Whitewashed tiles
ABOVE: *Moslem and Christian, nobleman and conquistador, farmer and peasant, each made their own contribution to the country buildings of Extremadura, Castilla La Mancha and the Levante. These two elements, tiles and whitewash, came from the Moslems.*

Las Hurdes
RIGHT: *Walls as well as roofs are faced with tiles on remote houses high in Las Hurdes. The tiles, laid in interlocking rows, were tapered to one end, the shape attributed to their being originally moulded against the tile maker's thigh.*

Trujillo

LEFT: *In the land of wheat prairies and bull-rearing plains where storks' nests top inaccessible chimneys, the province of Cáceres is dotted with fifteenth-century palaces and sixteenth-century manor houses. They belonged to the nobility who gained their titles battling with the Moslems or conquering American Indians.*

coats of arms and the whitewashed houses of the small towns which hug the huge hillsides of the north have an undiscovered feel to them. In Las Hurdes, the impoverished communities of the hills used in 1932 as a back-cloth by the Spanish film maker Louis Buñuel for his Tierra Sin Pan, the Land without Bread, the local Hurdanos are supposed to have discovered the concept of Christianity only in the late-nineteenth century, so remote were they from civilisation. Their slate-and-whitewash houses cluster round the ubiquitous plaza, and the buildings in El Asegur, La Huetre and other villages in the area look much as they must have done a century ago. At Santibañez el Alto, some older stone houses are ancient enough to be, even today, windowless. In Miranda del Castañar, and among the cherry orchards surrounding Hervás to the east where the *aljama de judíos* (Jewish quarter) has been carefully preserved, the widespread eaves and balconies brimming with flowers on the sixteenth-century, half-timbered houses lean perilously over the streets. Until the crop was mechanised, the tobacco harvest was hung to dry beneath these overhanging storeys.

South of these sierra, the farmland towards Cáceres and Badajoz is more productive and the *fincas* (farms), fed by the Tajo and Guadiana, produce cork and cotton, wheat, tobacco, maize and sunflowers. In some quietly charming small towns and villages like Jerez de los Caballeros, Fregenal de la Sierra and Llerena, the whitewashed houses are as Andalucian as anything across the southern border.

Extremadura was a buffer zone between Moslem and Christian, its castles continually changing hands during the Reconquista. As the Moslems were driven out, the *caballeros* (knights) were given great tracts of land in Extremadura and Castilla La Mancha as a reward for their contribution to the war effort, and several groups of villages carried their feudal landlord's name. A future in the agricultural wastelands of Extremadura looked less promising to the second or bastard sons of these erstwhile war lords than a trip overseas into the fabled lands so talked about since Christopher Columbus' return. Many rode down to join the ships sailing to the new world from Palos de la Frontera near Huelva; in fact a third of the Spanish *conquistadores* (conquerors) came from Badajoz or Cáceres.

119

Conquistadores homes

RIGHT: *Trujillo, said to have sired twenty American nations, is filled with baronial mansions, built by conquerors and colonists, the Indianos who left for Latin America and returned to plough their booty into grand town houses.*

Stylish loggias

RIGHT: *The Indianos built their homes of local stone, but included sixteenth- and seventeenth-century features such as loggias and corner windows with balconies. They also followed the local practice of highlighting their windows with whitewash.*

The soldiers of fortune who conquered Mexico, Peru, Chile and Florida, men such as Cortés, Pizarro, De Soto and De Balboa, were all Extremadurans who carried their Christianity to the new world and also settled the Americas with a string of Extremaduran place names. Those who survived with plunder for the return journey built resplendent palaces in their home towns and renamed streets and buildings with Latin American names. Trujillo, the capital of the returning conquistadores, Cáceres and the surrounding villages abound with *casas solariegas* (noble palaces) with their regal *blasones* (coats of arms) set over the doors and the Moslem courtyards with their tiled basins and fountains fed from *aljibes* (underground water stores). Even the chimneys on the roof of the Palacio de los Duques de San Carlos, a former nunnery in Trujillo, were shaped like Aztec pyramids.

Further south towards Badajoz were farming communities such as those on Tierra de Barros (literally, muddy land), dependent on the olive crops, cork forests, figs and vineyards. The high architecture of the towns and the

villages owes more to the Gothic and Renaissance than the Moslem styles. Spain's Renaissance architecture, profoundly influenced by Juan de Herrera, enjoyed a brief but sparkling romance with the Plateresque style, finely detailed masonry decoration which took its name from the delicate craft work of another kind, *plateros* (silversmiths). In and around Badajoz it was the Portuguese Manueline rather than the Spanish Plateresque which made its mark for in the territorial struggles between the neighbouring countries, Tierra de Barros often fell under Portuguese rule.

Badajoz did not enjoy a peaceful past. Regarded by the Portuguese as the key to their kingdom, the Badajoz region was a frequent victim in tug-of-war battles. Farming in a battle zone was not easy, but there was worse to come. The War of Independence was triggered by Napoleon's brother Joseph taking the title of King of Spain in 1805. The people of Madrid responded by cutting as many French throats as they could find and the French retaliated with cannon shot in a bloodbath which became the subject of some of Goya's darkest paintings. During the ensuing war thousands of British soldiers died storming Badajoz. There was, in 1936, a second massacre during the Civil War, when Republicans were lined up in the local bullring and shot.

Military disasters, corruption in high places and the eviction of the Moriscos debilitated the country. One of the war victims was Miguel de Cervantes. Born in 1547 and in captivity before he had reached his thirties (he was sold into slavery in Algiers) he devoted his time to writing and unsuccessfully avoiding the debtor's prison. He died destitute in 1616 as his book, *Don Quixote*, arrived in pirated editions on the street. Cervantes chose one of the bleaker parts of the kingdom, La Mancha, for the setting of his story of the idealistic knight errant fighting for his beliefs. In doing so he made the humble windmill the most famous vernacular building in Spain, and famed throughout the world.

Depending on natural elements and the hard physical labour of the miller, wind- and water-mills were among the most energy-efficient buildings. The water mill, whether used for grinding corn or pumping water around irrigation channels, simply required a building, a drive wheel and a

Villanueva de la Vera

RIGHT: *La Vera, a fertile valley of tobacco, cherry and orange trees, is fed by the gargantas, streams which run off the Sierra de Gredos into the valley. At Villanueva painted shutters shield the house from the heat.*

Spring fed

RIGHT: *If the rains fail or too little
snow falls in winter, the crops of the
Vera are in jeopardy. Each spring, city
visitors from Madrid come to admire the
sea of cherry blossom which surrounds
house-proud villages like
Valverde de la Vera.*

supply of water. But the windmill, a building with moving parts, was more complicated: it needed to be turned to catch the prevailing winds and to be sufficiently tall for its canvas sails to clear the ground. The moving parts of the mills in La Mancha were mounted in revolving cone-shaped rooves, which were turned by pulling or pushing a long sapling.

Agricultural mechanisation has made most windmills redundant and many of those that remain in and around Tomelloso, Campo de Criptana, Alcázar de San Juan and Consuegra (the home of the world's largest saffron harvest), have been converted to other uses including, in one case, a tourist information office.

In an effort to develop tourism and to wean visitors far away from the seductive if overcrowded charms of the coast the government in the 1950s started converting old buildings into *paradores* (state-run hotels – from *parada*, a stopping place). There are around a hundred paradores, some of them serving as living museums of Spanish medieval life. In Oropesa, north of Guadalupe, the battlemented castle provided a dramatic setting for a parador. Nearby at Lagartera, the village women supported their families

Garganta la Olla

RIGHT: *Limewashed houses grace the old mountain village of Garganta near the Monasterio de Yuste. Colour had practical as well as aesthetic use – in the sixteenth century, blue traditionally denoted the Casa de Putas or brothel.*

by embroidering peasant style skirts, tablecloths and silk hangings. In Guadalupe where the craft economy was based around smelting copper for jugs and pots, the local houses were built out across the cobbled streets, the great timber sills of the upper floors supported on weathered tree trunks cut in the days when building timber was more plentiful than today.

Walls of village houses were built in whatever was locally available, that is, timber frame, freestone or brick, and finished with whitewash. Where there were no suitable building materials, or where the householder was too poor to purchase them, tapia or pisé came into its own. Pisé was introduced to the French by the Romans and is a traditional building technique in Asia and Africa as well as southern Europe.

The method involved forming a foundation of rubble or brick and then throwing an earthy mixture of sand and gravel, with a little clay to bind the dirt, down between wooden shuttering boards. Sometimes broken glass was added to the mix, supposedly to prevent rats and mice tunnelling into the

Casa de Pescadores
RIGHT: *The round thatched cabañas in the Valle de la Vera still serve the community in which they were built.*

Outdoor life
RIGHT: *Not everyone could afford to roof their outdoor terrace, but a sheltering vine trained across timber supports served just as well. A flagstone floor was angled to drain rainwater away from the house.*

walls. A wooden pole or an iron rod fixed with a heart-shaped spear was used to pound the mixture with great force and even greater precision until all the air pockets had been removed and the dry mix was compacted into a solid mass. An even harder mix could be made by adding a little cement wherethis was available.

Under the hot Castilian sun, the walls rose rapidly – a man could build up to his own height in a day – although a sudden thunder storm would ruin a day's work, turning the brick-hard wall into a mud bath. Once the walls were in place, brick or wood frames were built in for the door and windows and the earthen sides weatherproofed with clay and painted with copious quantities of limewash. A skirting coat of tar was painted around the building; this was intended to deter passing farm animals from licking away the tapi and was most effective.

The sun lifts over Valencia and Murcia each morning, hence the name, the Levante (literally, rising). The region stretches from Catalonia down the Mediterranean coast to the Andalucian border. During the late-sixteenth century, approximately one-third of the people were Moslems and until their expulsion in 1609 their farming expertise was important in helping to make the provinces of Castellón, Valencia, Alicante and Murcia the most fertile and productive areas of Spain.

The lemon groves of Murcia's *vega* (fertile plain), the date palms of Elche in Alicante, their fronds harvested for Palm Sunday worshippers each year, and the paddy fields of rice in Valencia's irrigated farmscape contributed to the city of Valencia becoming the third largest metropolis in Spain after Madrid and Barcelona.

The Costa del Azahar, the Orange Blossom Coast, and the Costa Blanca, the White Coast, have lost many of their traditional country buildings to the twentieth-century expansion of tourist hotels. Elsewhere the vernacular architecture ranges from basic thatched *barracas* (little whitewashed cabins with steep thatched roofs) in La Albufera to the medieval houses in Sagunto's Jewish quarter. Jewish history claims Sagunto, north of Valencia, as their first settlement in all Spain, and their later medieval houses have survived in the Judería. Roman columns supporting some of the arcades in

Arid plains

RIGHT: *On the hot arid plains of Albacete province – Al Basite meant 'the plain' to the Arabs – are houses which have been hollowed out of the side of the cliffs.*

the plaza date to around 200 BC when Hannibal captured the town – but only after the inhabitants had committed mass suicide. South of Valencia the local villages of La Albufera, from the Arabic meaning a small sea, have maintained their barracas, some on stilt foundations.

Houses in the bastide-like villages of El Maestrazgo on the borders of Aragón and the province of Castellón, fortified for the fight against the Moslems, have maintained a distinctly medieval atmosphere. Valencia's economic and artistic flowering in the fifteenth century gave rise to a series of dignified Gothic mansions, and to networks of village workshops where

Guadalest

RIGHT: *The sixteenth century Moslem town of Guadalest was built into the limestone escapements of the Sierra de Aitana, reached by an archway cut through the rock. The sparkling houses of limestone and whitewash stand surrounded by terraces of olives and almonds between the sea and the mountains.*

The Levante

RIGHT: *The villages of the Levante are scattered across some of the richest agricultural land in Europe, farmed by Moriscos, Moslems who had converted to Christianity, until their expulsion in 1609.*

Alternative views
LEFT: *Some of the houses hollowed out of the rock face at Alcala del Jucar have tunnels running through the rock. They opened out on to balconies overlooking the far side of the cliffs.*

CASTILLA LA MANCHA · EXTREMADURA

local craftspeople worked their gold, their silver and wrought ironwork, as well as their embroidery and ceramics.

When Malagueño potters from Andalucía migrated to Valencia they sparked off an exuberant form of Hispano-Moresque ceramics as Christians and Moslems worked together. But the traditional green motifs of the thirteenth and fourteenth centuries and the blue of the fifteenth ground to a halt when the Moslems left.

The industry was revived in the eighteenth century particularly at Alcora in the Valencian mountains where, until it was occupied by French forces in the early-nineteenth century and later destroyed by British forces, the local porcelain was patronised by both royalty and peasant alike. Valencian plates painted with simple floral or arabesque designs could be found on the scrubbed pine table of every casa in the region long afterwards.

But life would never have been the same in the Levante without the work of Valencian carpenters who every year hoarded their wood shavings for a great bonfire on the eve of the feast of St Joseph in March. The tradition developed into the building of the *fallas*, huge cardboard and papier mâché figures burned in an orgy of flame and fireworks during the fiesta. Not for nothing are the Valencian buildings marked with small white-and-blue plaques – a sign that they are insured against accidental fire.

A more traditional use of the wood fire was to cook the Valencian dish *paella*, made from locally grown rice, green beans and meat. Customarily, paella is served to the spectators who gather at the various village fiestas to witness the annual mock battles which take place between Moslems and Christians, a centuries-old commemoration of the long hard fight for this rich agricultural region, an area regarded by both sides as the fertile jewel in the Spanish crown.

With its blue tiled church roofs, its thatched farmhouses and its *clara*, the clean, clear local light so loved by artists, the Levante lies a long way from the glowering hills and deep green olive groves of Extremadura to the west. In many respects the region shares considerably more of the character and colour of its southern neighbour, Andalucía, the place which for many centuries the Moslem civilisation truly regarded as heaven on earth.

ᴀNDALUCÍA

T URN YOUR COLLAR up against the spring chill and stand on the Sierra Nevada south of Granada – the region below you has a pulse which has touched the world. The *cante jondo*, the haunting song at the heart of the flamenco, the coup de grâce in the breath-held stillness of the bullfight, the contemplative calm of the Alhambra palace gardens . . . these emotional moments have become common currency in the portrayal of Spanish daily life.

Yet until the region was united under the Catholic monarchs in 1492, the Sevillanos of the west who were endowed with wild gypsy charms were just about a race apart from the Almerienses to the east where in the recent past the women still veiled themselves against passing strangers. There was room enough for the different andaluces to live side by side because Andalucía is as big as it is beautiful.

Called Baetica by the Romans, Andalucía occupies almost one-sixth of the Spanish peninsula and has the highest population of all Spain's regions. The community's seven million citizens are concentrated in the great cities of Cádiz, Málaga, Seville, Córdoba and Granada rather than in the quiet country backwaters, where donkeys have yet to be usurped by cars, where limpid *balsas* (spring-fed reservoirs) irrigate crops and serve as informal swimming pools during long summer evenings noisy with barking dogs and crowing cocks rather than the cacophony of television sets.

Andalucía, or Al Andalus, as the Moslems christened it, is separated into eight provinces each with a capital of the same name. The provincial names, Huelva, Seville, Cádiz, Córdoba, Jaén, Málaga, Granada and Almería, ring with Spanish romance. Andalucía lines up along both the blue Mediterranean Sea and the rolling grey Atlantic Ocean and it was this seascape which brought international fame to Andalucía. Although less than one-fifth of the coastline is developed, villages and former malarial swamps have turned into fun for some, harrowing tourist traps for others.

Andalucía

LEFT: *Arcos de la Frontera built on a crag overlooking the Guadalete river in the province of Cádiz was, as the name suggests, a frontier town during battles between the Christians and the Moslems.*

The ancient fiefdoms are physically divided up by two chains of horn toothed mountains and by the luxuriant delta of the great Guadalquivir River which rises in the Cazorla National Park to the east and runs west, passing through Córdoba and Seville before emptying into the Atlantic. In the north the Guadalquivir passes along the Sierra Morena's southern flanks which mark off the borders between Andalucía and the Castilian plateau. The Beatic Chain, veined with mineral deposits and clothed in oak, mastic and arbutus trees, includes the Serranía de Ronda, the Sierra de Ubrique and the Sierra Nevada where Mulhacén is the highest mountain on the Spanish mainland. Named in honour of Muley Hassan, father of the last Moslem king, Boabdil, Mulhacén is one of Andalucía's Moslem landmarks.

The farmers of Andalucía see their countryside as a maze of small plains and valleys wedged in by mountains or laid out along the coastline. What little arable land there is has been cultivated to produce not only the Mediterranean staples of olives, cereals and vines, but rice, cotton, sugar cane and citrus fruits, and to breed fighting bulls.

Andalucía was conquered by the Moslems, crossing the Atlantic from Morocco and North Africa in 711 AD. When they were vanquished by the Christians during the reconquest they left in their wake not only the characteristic white hill towns, but also exotic architectural details: the *sebka* (intricate plasterwork) which embellishes walls and arches like petrified lace; the horseshoe arches shaped like giant keyholes; coffered artesonado ceilings, each star-shaped section as richly decorated as a sixteenth-century jewellery box; *alicatado*, the glazed-tiled skirtings and wainscots which are always cool to the touch however hot the day; delicate ajimez windows where the twin, semi-circular arches are carried on slim colonettes; and Hand of Fátima door knockers, symbols of Islamic sympathy, gracefully extended to the house visitor.

There were three major periods of Hispano-Moslem architecture, each related to the reign of successive Arab dynasties and to the towns which became their footholds in Spain. The earliest, the Caliphate, related to Córdoba and the city mosque. Typified by *alcázares* (palaces), the *alcazabas* (castles), and the *mezquitas* (mosques) and their minarets, the Caliphate style

Inner calm
RIGHT: *The inner courtyard, surrounded by cool arcades and focused on a playful fountain, was a central feature of Moslem life. This is the Palace of the Marqués de la Gomera at Osuna near Seville.*

incorporated red-and-white, stone-and-brick arches, courtyards with a pool for ritual washing, and a *mihrab*, the prayer niche in the prayer room which marked the direction of Mecca.

Between the twelfth and thirteenth centuries the influence was Almohad, based on Seville, and characterised by a more restrained and simplified approach to decoration in buildings such as the Giralda, once a minaret. Almohad features included artesonado and azulejos, both of which were carried to Aragón by the Mudéjares.

The last group, the Nasrid period from the fourteenth to the fifteenth centuries, was based in Granada and epitomised by the Alhambra and its innovative decoration where door and window surrounds acted as a focal point for the design and ornamentation of the rest of the room.

Elements from all three periods and the later Mudéjar are to be found on a string of old palaces in and around Granada, Córdoba and Spain's fourth largest city, Seville. Many of the baronial homes stood as the centrepiece of estates given by grateful Catholic monarchs to Christian nobles for their

efforts in the Reconquista. Then there are the *carmenes*, country villas of the hills around Granada, where the house itself seems subordinate to the garden, overflowing with bougainvillaea, jasmine and fruit trees.

Hundreds of such houses have fallen derelict or suffered insensitive restorations which have destroyed all trace of their past. Those that survive exhibit an eclectic mix of architectural styles and furnishings. Castilian ironsmiths might have manufactured the wrought iron balcony over the main entrance or the fluted columns which carry the trellis of vines in the shaded courtyard, and Mudéjar craftsmen would have been employed to execute the delicate stucco cornices and the vibrant tiles of the floors, pools and fountains. Huge heraldic tapestries hung on the walls of the principal salones side by side with carved statues of Inca figures, celebrating the close association with the Americas. An eastern carpet might be spread over the tiles in the cool entrance hall, and pride of place given to a heavy, carved chest of Spanish oak, while the decorative bowls or burnished copper pots, standing on its carved lid, will have unmistakable Moslem origins.

Since the Mudéjares worked their crafts under Christian rule in Andalucía long after the fifteenth century Reconquista, their handiwork also survives on the more humble architecture of the region. Three factors dictate the look of these rural buildings: local climate, local produce and the size of the house owner's purse. In those parts of Andalucía where the village streets are too narrow or too steep to admit a car, and those where the family's mule is stabled along with the hens on the ground floor, the traditional houses look more or less as they must have done a century ago.

The casa, its adobe walls whitewashed once or twice a year, may have had its windows enlarged, but it is still shuttered against the sun or hung with a woven esparto mat draped over the balcony to let in any breeze. Inside, beaten earth or pebbles laid in diagonal or chevron patterns lined the ground floors, and terra-cotta tiles, made from clay and crushed almond husks, formed the floors above. Other features common to most Andalucian interiors included low beamed ceilings, little stoves set in tiled recesses in the thick walls, narrow bands of *verduguillos* (tiles) edging shelves, steps and mantelpieces, and bright Talavera crockery.

Arcos de la Frontera

RIGHT: *Taken from the Moslems two centuries before the fall of Granada in 1492, Moslem and Renaissance buildings sit side by side in Arcos de la Frontera. The Mudéjar church is flanked by castle walls on one side and the plunging river valley on the other.*

Home work

LEFT: *The poverty which dogged Andalucía for centuries was partly alleviated by opening up the southern coast to tourism. But in the interior, the simple craftsman's home still doubles as his workshop.*

Winter warmth

LEFT: *The southern winter might be short, but the nights are long and cold especially in the Sierra Nevada where Mulhacén lords it as the highest mountain in Spain. Here the milking stool and rush seated chair stand near the warmth of the wash house boiler.*

Outside rooms

LEFT: *The traditional focus of family life for most of the year in Andalucía was the terrace outside the back door. Whether it was a small town patio or here in a garden courtyard near Cádiz, water has been a central feature since the days of the Moslems.*

Talavera ceramics, centred on Talavera de la Reina near Toledo in Castilla La Mancha, became a household name when the tile makers, who had been manufacturing their distinctive hand painted blue-and-yellow tile designs, turned their attention to pots, bowls and other domestic ware. Hardly a house in all Spain was without some piece of Talavera pottery, made by pressing the wet clay with carved wooden moulds before glazing – another craft with its roots in Andalucía itself.

The Koran forbade the use of precious metals in decoration, prohibiting the representation of animals or people in architectural ornamentation. The ever resourceful Moslems turned to the ceramicist who in turn responded by developing his craft into an art form. Unglazed tiles had been used since Roman times; the Moslems introduced the art of sealing the clay with thin coatings of glass. The composition of these iridescent metallic glazings was a secret guarded closely by the Malagueños, the migrant Moslem potters and painters who settled Málaga in the thirteenth century.

From the giant *tinajas* (earthern wine containers), which today are often filled with flowers, to ornate tiled altars and public squares, ceramic work dominates both public and private places. Although many of the old crafts and customs are quietly disappearing, potters still fire their clay in kilns designed by the last of the Moslems.

Moslem architecture reached its zenith with the Nasrid Alhambra in Granada. The palace is conventional in its lay-out of three sections: one where the everyday business affairs of government were conducted, the next where visiting dignitaries would be entertained; and the third which was devoted to the private apartments of the ruler and his entourage. What made the Alhambra a masterpiece was the decoration – the stucco and ceramics, the lace-like plasterwork and the delicately carved capitals of the columns. The basic building was rough rubble, plaster and brick, for no Nasrid prince ever expected his handiwork to last long, but the result was a sensual synthesis of stone and plaster, wood and water.

The great mosque at Córdoba to the north was another celebration of Islamic style with candy-stripped arches and a lavishly decorated mihrab. A mihrab was often designed with a shell-shaped dome to amplify the sound

Village blacksmith

LEFT: *Iron forging is an ancient Iberian craft and many of the wrought iron grills which protect the country doors and windows of southern Spain are still made by the village blacksmith.*

Pueblos blancos

LEFT: *Whitewashed walls and terra cotta tiled roofs decorate the pueblos blancos, the white villages of Andalucía. Like Caseres, many cling to steep hillsides topped by castles.*

of the single voice at prayer. With such riches as these on their doorstep, the humbler homes of Andalucía could not resist the influence of the east.

Córdoba was the meeting point of three civilisations, the Islamic, Christian and Jewish people. It stands on the banks of the Guadalquivir River between the northern *haciendas*, country estates still laid out on the rectangular Roman lines, and the olive groves and wheat fields of the south. Some of the finest Andalucian cortijos, their terra-cotta tiled roofs and whitewashed facades shimmering under the southern sun in an almost earthy display of indigenous craft, pattern these landscapes.

Frigiliana

LEFT: *One of the most atmospheric of the pueblos blancos, Frigiliana lies close to the Costa del Sol near Málaga. Many of the architectural elements, from the reja and the flower filled balconies to the patterned floors and decorated nailheads of the doors, are brought together in this former Phoenician settlement.*

Ronda

Top floor terraces and steep tiled roofs characterise the view of La Ciudad, Ronda's old walled town. A picturesque enclave of narrow alleys and iron balconies, Ronda was occupied by the Moslems until 1485. Three hundred years later, the neoclassical bullring was built; it is now one of the oldest in Spain.

Inside, the furniture in the first-floor kitchen was covered in best Cordoban leather, tooled and gilded, and the walls nestled with mihrab-like alcoves filled with the green-and-blue pottery of Granada or the red crockery of Guadix. The bedrooms, built on the ground floor for coolness, would open out on to arched cloisters which surrounded a fountain-filled courtyard or *alberca* (reservoir).

The troglodyte quarter of Guadix east of Granada represented the other end of the social scale. These cave houses were hollowed out of the soft, tufa rock. The stone-faced entrances are whitewashed and conical chimneys emerge bearing a television aerial or two on the path above.

Rural Andalucía has been dogged by poverty and many Andaluces still cannot afford some of the basic twentieth-century benefits which their coastal cousins, capitalising on the coastal tourist trade, managed to acquire several years ago.

In the western part of Huelva province, the quieter face of Andalucía is represented by Aracena, Alajar, Jabugo and other places which are dotted

Historical traces
LEFT: *Like so many towns in Andalucía, Ronda carries the region's history on the face of its buildings. Traces of the old mosque and Mudéjar minaret survive in the Collegiate church which replaced it while Inca-like carvings decorate the walls of one of its town palaces.*

with brick minarets and hills studded with chestnuts and olive trees. Between Huelva and Seville the Doñana National Park consists of southern Europe's finest marshlands which preserve the tortoise, golden eagle and flamingo and conserve old-style primitive huts roofed with branches and used as shelters by pine-kernel gatherers.

For most of the year, the streets of sand, white walls and terra-cotta roofs of El Rocío, north of Doñana, are deathly quiet, but for three days they erupt into action when the Whitsun festival fills the village with upwards of a million pilgrims. They ride in, their mule-drawn waggons decorated with garlands of flowers, their horsemen wearing broad brimmed hats, short jackets, scarlet cummerbunds and leather chaps and sharing their fine Andalucian saddles with señoritas in full-skirted flamenco dresses. Three days later, after an extravagant display of rural celebration, they ride out again and leave the place in peace for another year.

The towns and villages to the east of El Rocío formed one of the frontiers between Moslem and Christian, as the Frontera suffixes to their names shows. And Jerez de la Frontera produced the name sherry, from the English pronunciation of its Spanish name, xeres. The bodegas of the sherry companies and the mansions of their Anglo-Spanish owners at nearby Puerto de Santa María make an elegant contribution to the local architecture, as do the flower-filled patios and whitewashed alleyways in Córdoba to the north.

At Baeza near Ubeda in Jaén the sixteenth-century houses are built of darkened limestone. Many of the stone-faced houses which look over the cliffs at Hornos, further east, are similarly free of whitewash. In Las Alpujarras, one of the more inaccessible parts of Andalucía, the tide of whitewash gradually creeping through the town and village buildings is relatively recent. Owners and managers of the courtly old hotels in the spa town of Lanjarón, which exports its mineral waters throughout Spain, would have regarded whitewash as the paint of the poor — there was little whitewash to be seen on the neighbouring Alpujarras houses when the hotels were constucted at the turn of the century. Built of grey rubble the Alpujarras home took a level roof of chestnut or ash beams, overlaid with split cane or chestnut matting. Flat stone tiles were carried by the timbers

Sierra Nevada

and a layer of *launa* (local grey grit) spread over the stones. If the job was done under a waning moon, it was said that the launa would guarantee a waterproof finish.

Throughout Andalucía and much of southern Spain, whitewash is the most distinctive mark on these southern buildings. The strikingly pretty pueblos blancos are widespread in Caseres, east of Gibraltar, in Níjar, north east of Almeria, where the villagers carry on the craft of *jarapas*, weaving thick hangings and bedspreads, and in Ronda where the father of modern bullfighting, Curro Romero, was born. Mojácar is known locally as the Pueblo Inglés because of the number of British people who have moved into this Moslem-style village of flat roofed houses and rooftop verandahs.

White has always been the prevailing Mediterranean colour, partly because it reflected the light but mostly because it was cheap to make, requiring only chalk dust, size made from boiled strips of leather, and a binding agent made from milk. Simple limewashes were used as exterior and interior decoration. They were made by burning quarried limestone in

Moriscos

Southern scenes

LEFT: *Crisp white villages, churches perched on dizzy heights and the bright blue of the Andalucian sky characterise the scenery of southern Spain.*

kilns to produce quicklime which was then dumped in a pit in the back yard and mixed with water. Tallow from melted down animal fat was added to give the limewash a longer lasting finish, and all manner of secretive, local recipes, some insisting on the inclusion of egg yolks, salt and wine, were developed to improve the mix.

The seventeenth-century costumes of the bull fighters are but one example of the Spaniard's zest for strong, carnival colours. Country buildings tend to be shaded with earth colours, the pigments ranging from bullock blood and plant dye to burnt earths of ochre and umber. The colours also change with the regions – pale greens and pastel blues inland in northern Spain, brighter cobalt blues and alizarin greens along the coastline. On the central plains Indian yellows, raw siennas, earthy reds and terra-cotta browns abound. There are vibrant colour schemes on the Mediterranean coast, where long ago Phoenicians learned to boil murex snail shells for their purple dye, and where South American gold is sewn into tapestries or gilded on church statues. Finally, there is the whitewash, used sparingly to highlight the windows on a Pyreneen farmhouse or lavished by bucketful on Andalucian pueblos. Without it, Andalucía under a midday sun would look a little drab; with it, the country buildings glitter like silver.

When, in the fifteeth century, Boabdil, the last of the Nasrid rulers, finally surrendered the city keys of Granada to his Christian conquerors, he left with his retinue by the pass known as Ultimo Suspiro del Moro, the Moor's Last Sigh. According to the legend he was berated by his mother who told him: 'You do well to weep like a woman for what you failed to defend like a man.' Bidding goodbye to all the visual treasures of the Spanish countryside for ever would make any man weep.

GLOSSARY

adobe: sun-dried clay brick

ajimez: twin-arched window

alberca: simple reservoir in courtyard

alcazaba: castle

alcázar: fortified place

alicatado: section of wall tiled to form geometric pattern

aljamas de judios: Jewish quarters

arquitectura negra: black architecture

artesonado: carved wooden ceilings

ayuntamiento: town hall

azulejos: glazed ceramic tiles

balsa: spring-fed reservoir

barraca: small whitewashed cabin with steep thatched roof

barro cocido: glazed earthenware

bodega: wine cellar

caballero: horseman

cabaña: hut, cabin

cabo: cape (topog.)

caliphate: (arcitectural) style developed in cordoba under the Moslem caliphate

cañadas: grazing routes of the meseta (q.v.)

cante jondo: song at heart of flamenco

carmen: country villa in Granada district of Andalucía

casa: house

casas de la malicia: 'houses of wickedness'

casa solariega: noble palace

Castellano: the Castillian language; a general term for Spanish national language

castillo: castle

Cierzo, El: north wind

cigarrál: country house, villa in the district of Toledo

Conquistador: conqueror

coroza: waterproof cape

cuerda seca: dry cord technique used in firing ceramic tiles

encierro: bull running

escudo: coat of arms

esgrafiado: decorative design etched in plaster and cement walls

esparto: woven grass mat

Extremenos: person from Extremadura

falla: large papier mâché figure

finca: house in country

flamenco: formal dance derived from gypsy and Arab sources

Gallego: the Galician language; a person from Galicia

hidalgo: nobleman or gentleman (literally: the son of somebody)

hórreo: corn granary in Galicia and Asturias

huerta: irrigated area

huerto de verduras: vegetable or kitchen garden

jarapas: weaving technique particularly of thick hangings and bedspreads

jerez: sherry

launa: grey grit of Las Alpujarras, Andalucía

loza dorada: ceramics technique where designs are painted over a background colour

manxa: Arabic term for the dry land of La Mancha

maragoto: muleteer

meseta: broad elevated plain; the central tableland of the Spanish mainland

mezquita: mosque

mirador: balcony window

molino: windmill

morillo: firedog

Moriscos: Moslems who adopted Christianity

Mozárabes: Christians who adopted Islam

Mudéjar: architectural work of Moslems under Christian rule

Nasrid: prince, also architectural style

orujo: Galician brandy

palloza: circular hut constructed of granite and topped with conical roof of thatch

parador: state-run hotel

pazo: Galician country house

pisé: method of building with dry, rammed earth

platero: silversmith

porrón: glass wine jar with the spout at the base

pueblo: village

pueblos blancos: villages of white washed houses

rancho: ranch

refugio: refuge

reja: iron grille or grating

ría: fjord-like cove

río: river

salón: drawing room

sebka: plasterwork decoration

sierra: mountain range

tapia: see pisé

tinaja: large clay wine container

toro bravo: fighting bull

tramontana: north wind in Catalonia

vega: fertile plain

vendimia: autumn grape harvest

verduguillo: narrow band of tiles

vieira: scallop

zuecos: clogs

INDEX

ACKNOWLEDGEMENTS

I owe my thanks to many people: Abby and Rosie for their patience;
Roger Calow, Chelsey Fox, Anne Middle, Simon Mole, David and
Catherine Petts, Viv Ray, Richard Sidwell, Viv Southorn and Nic Ward
for their contributions. I am especially indebted to
Santi Dominguez for his native Galician knowledge.

Traditional Houses Of Rural Spain is dedicated to
Peggy Laws and her spirit of adventure.